An early twentieth century postcard by W. Phillips of Ivybridge.

RECOLLECTIONS OF IVYBRIDGE AND DISTRICT

Originating largely in the eighteenth century, the town of Ivybridge grew to a small but thriving community during the nineteenth. With its paper mills and other local industries, governed by its own Urban Council, and with a wide range of shops and other tradesmen, the town was very much a self-contained centre and for most local people journeys, even as far as Plymouth, were the exception rather than the rule.

For the first fifty years of the present century the town showed little growth and remained something of a rural backwater, enlivened only by such events as the wartime stationing of U.S. troops here. Post-war growth, starting slowly, has accelerated with the building of new housing estates and the population has increased several fold with an increasing proportion of workers commuting to Plymouth or elsewhere. Although the pattern of facilities in the town has changed, much of the old centre of Ivybridge, despite some unsympathetic shopfronts in Fore Street, remains as it was eighty or more years ago as some of these photographs show.

The pictures are from the collections of Mr. A. A. Rogers, Mr. F. Hoare, Mr. R. Vincent and others with postcards and prints from my own set. To those who generously allowed the use of their pictures and to those for whom I am indebted for information, grateful thanks. As for the text, I accept full responsibility for errors and omissions. Identifications of people are as indicated in the text or by F. Hoare/A. Rogers.

© A. D. Barber, 1981.

This version of the book is virtually as originally published, presenting the work of AD Barber.
There are now additional pages at the back providing information about the publisher, Arthur L Clamp.

The republishing project is being managed by Arthur's grandson, Steven Gibson. We aim to find all the research that he was involved in publishing, preserving it for the next generation as part of 'The Clamp Collection'.

IVYBRIDGE

Ivybridge grew up in the corners of the four ancient parishes of Cornwood, Harford, Ugborough and Ermington where they met at the old bridge. The church was in Cornwood, the London Hotel in Harford, the Sportsman's Arms (Grocer's Arms) in Ugborough and most of the village itself in Ermington.

The name "Ponte Ederoso" is first recorded from 1250 and "Ivybrugge" in 1292 but these refer to the river crossing rather than a distinct settlement. It was the turnpike, and later the paper mills that led to the growth of a small village such that a church was provided in 1789. An ecclesiastical district of Ivybridge was formed in 1836 but civil government remained split between the four parishes until the 1870s when a Sanitary District with an Ivybridge Local Board was formed.

It was in 1894 that urban sanitary districts became urban district councils, Ivybridge Urban District Council was born and all formal connection with the old parishes was severed.

The Council, with its office in Highland Street and later Fore Street lasted until 1935 when it was absorbed into that of Plympton St. Mary Rural District and Ivybridge reduced to the status of a parish.

IVYBRIDGE COUNCILLORS INSPECT THE RESERVOIR

In this picture, taken at the Harford reservoir, probably sometime after the First World War may be seen, from left to right: —, Dr. Trumper, Mr. Venn, Mr. Hands, Mr. Freeman, Mr. H. Vincent (in cap), Mr. Weekes, Mr. Bill Martin, Mr. "Bunzy" Phillips, Mr. Bert Blight (Blight & Scoble). The reservoir had been opened by the U.D.C. in June 1916, having cost some £17,000. Names by R. W. H. Vincent.

OLD PRINTS OF IVYBRIDGE

1780: Detail of an engraving by F. Chesham after Paul Sandby, R.A., showing the old bridge and what we may presume later became the London Hotel.

1832: Detail of an engraving by H. Wallis after G. B. Campion showing what is presumably the Devonport stage outside the "Rogers Arms" (now Grosvenor House). Fore Street is in the background.

ST. JOHN'S CHURCH

First licenced for divine service in 1789 and consecrated in 1835, the Chapel of St. John consisted of a western tower and nave to which, apparently, in 1835 a North aisle had been added. There was a western porch on the building which was described as of "rubble, roughly plastered on the outside". Other features, it would seem were a stained glass East window, plaster mouldings and ornaments on the ceilings, a gallery and a canopy over the pulpit.

In order to provide a new building, a committee was set up in 1876, chaired by Lord Blachford. Con-

Ruins of old St. Johns.

temporary accounts speak of the old church as "unsuitable for restoration or enlargement" or "having been built during days of faint devotion to a most unecclesiastical design".

The foundation stone of the new St. John's was laid in June 1881, the new building was consecrated a year later, and it became the parish church in January, 1883. In 1887 the North aisle was added but no tower was ever built; the monuments, altar and font were transferred from the old building.

After the opening of the new church the interior and roof of old St. John's were removed and in 1890 the Vestry meeting proposed to demolish the rest of the building. Following a petition of more than 300 signatures, the bishop commissioned an architect's report and refused permission for demolition. The "ruins" remained a picturesque feature of Ivybridge for a further 35 years until taken down, apparently to provide building stone, in 1925.

The chancel of the new church was refitted in memory of Lord Blachford (d. 1889); the East window dates from 1890. The picture shows the appearance of this part of the church before the erection of the screen (1910) and cross (1925) by the Bayley family of Highlands.

THE ROMAN CATHOLIC CHURCH AT CADLEIGH

A Catholic convent and school were established at Cadleigh early in the twentieth century. The picture probably dates from those early years. Methodism in Ivybridge dates from 1812 when the first chapel was completed, and an Independent (Congregational) chapel from the 1840s.

A view of the old viaduct with Beacon Villas and Woodhaye prior to 1893.

Two views of the station and Western Beacon.

THE SOUTH DEVON RAILWAY

The broad gauge South Devon Railway (later Great Western), based on the designs of I. K. Brunel, reached Ivybridge in 1848. The viaduct was one of the outstanding engineering features of the line, single track 252 yards long, and of stone and timber construction.

Despite the advantages of the 7' 0½" gauge the Great Western eventually fell in with the rest of Britain and over the weekend 20th - 23rd May, 1892, the remaining broad gauge track, including the South Devon line was converted to standard 4' 8½". In 1893 the line was doubled and new stone viaducts constructed at Ivybridge and Cornwood. Ivybridge station was enlarged and a goods station added.

The station in the early 1900s.

The remains of the pillars of Brunel's viaduct still stand in the woods above the present one. The view from Ivybridge station was described as "as fine a view as almost any other in the country" but its site was a long way up from the town centre.

View from the station showing the paper mills.

Post-war increases in car ownership and competition from bus services made the future of stations such as Ivybridge very doubtful. By 1958 an average of only 16 alighting and 22 joining passengers each day was reported and final closure of the station took place on 2nd March, 1959. The signal box survived until the early 1970s.

The viaduct and Henlake Down.

THE GREAT BLIZZARD OF 1891

On the night of 9th March, 1891, a combination of snow and a gale force wind affected much of South West England. A full share of the effects of the blizzard was felt by Ivybridge.

Many trains were snowed up including the 6.50 p.m. up from Plymouth which ran into a snowdrift in Langham cutting. Forty or more passengers were stuck in the train overnight without food and it was only the next morning that a rescue party from Ivybridge made it to the train. Many of the passengers were hospitably accommodated by Miss Glanville at her house nearby.

STOWFORD PAPER MILLS

First constructed by William Dunsterville in 1785, passing through the Rivers, Fincher, Godfrey and Acland families the mills were purchased by John Allen of Plymouth in 1849. Increased production and mechanisation during the control of the Allen family built the mills up to be a major employer in Ivybridge with more than 200 people working there.

In 1910 the mills were sold to a syndicate including R. H. Clapperton. A serious fire, of somewhat mysterious origin, destroyed many of the buildings on 6th May, 1914, causing serious problems for workers then out of jobs.

The 1914 fire.

Rebuilt and back into production soon after the fire, the mills passed to Portals of Laverstoke in 1924 and then to Wiggins Teape (now part of Imperial Tobacco) in 1930. As recently as 1929 every postage stamp in Great Britain was printed on Ivybridge paper and it is specialisation that has meant the survival of the Mill.

The Mills about 1930.

VIEWS OF IVYBRIDGE (ABOUT 1910)

By the early years of the twentieth century Ivybridge had developed as a small town with its own market (present health centre site), police station (Highland Street), petty sessions (at one time in the London Hotel, later at the old chapel), masonic hall, institute, churches of several denominations and Urban Council.

These two pictures were taken by Headley Vincent, uncle of the present town mayor, showing views of the town before the First World War. W. H. Bowden started with bicycles and when motor cars arrived moved into the repair of these. On the opposite side of Western Road was Hoare's garage.

A picture taken by W. R. Gay of South Brent showing another view of Western Road. Smith's Tea House may be seen just behind the group of children (now estate agent's). For day trippers from Plymouth they would provide hot water, teapot, cups and saucers for twopence; the visitors brought their own tea.

Three views of Fore Street; most of this area had been built up before 1830. Before the 1914-18 War the roads were little more than mud on their surface, a Mr. Williams being employed by the Council to clear off the slurry from the road after wet weather — he also cleared up after the horses as well as assisting with refuse collection and driving the steam roller! For this he probably got a wage of less than eighteen shillings a week.

The picture above shows Phillips cycle shop; next to this was a general store and then F. A. Rutherford, the chemist whose speciality was Rutherford's Cough Mixture, sold for a shilling and costing, it was alleged, three halfpence to make.

The post office was originally in Western Road (now Sunnyside) but a new building in Fore Street (right) was opened about the turn of the century. Mail would arrive by train with an automatic drop at the viaduct. A postman would push his barrow up to the station (in the dark — no streetlamps were on) at 4 o'clock in the morning to collect the Ivybridge mail.

FURTHER VIEWS AROUND THE TOWN

Incorrectly labelled "Fore Street" this view of Erme Road, one of the oldest parts of the town, shows how little it has changed in the last seventy or eighty years. J. M. Randle, local doctor and medical officer, occupied the house now known as "Erme-side". Patients went up the side entrance where he kept his pony and trap and hence into the waiting room.

The new Wesleyan church was given by John Allen Snr. in 1875. The family were very active Methodists and would arrive for chapel in an open Victoria each Sunday morning. The old chapel is now the Town Hall. Grosvenor House (once the Rogers Arms) was a later residence of local doctors.

Factory Bridge, shown on this view, was the exit from the town to the Ermington road. Demolished in 1973 to make way for the Ivybridge by-pass (opened twenty years after first planned), no trace remains but the factory building on the left is now used by a sailmaker.

A view of the river in winter. The river, the woods, and the surrounding moorland have been features of the town which have attracted visitors and the view from the "new" (1820s) bridge to the old one is much photographed. It has been said that one necessary qualification to being considered a local boy is to have fallen, fully clothed, into the Erme between the two bridges.

The London Hotel, dating from the late eighteenth century, seems always to have been a social centre for the village — many a celebration, such as laying a foundation stone, seems to have been rounded off with an appropriate luncheon or tea at Mallett's London Hotel.

When the hotel was sold in 1903 it was described as having "coffee and commercial rooms, 5 sitting rooms, bar, smoking room, market room, 15 bedrooms, spacious ball and assembly room, billiard room" and "capital, well accustomed public bar known as the London Hotel Tap".

Victoria Park, once an area of rough ground known as Chapel Wood, was given to the town to celebrate the Jubilee of 1898.

An undated newspaper report of one jubilee celebration (1887 or 1897) tells of a celebration dinner in Chapel Woods at which 1,600 sat down. Sports, a bonfire on Western Beacon and presentation of commemorative medals to all the children (600) had been preceded by handbell ringers parading the streets at 4.30 a.m. and playing "God save the Queen".

RURAL LIFE AT THE TURN OF THE CENTURY

These pictures are based on prints from a set of plates taken by Charles Smallridge, author of the picture postcards shown on the previous page. They were found at Longtimbers some eighty years later by Mr. F. Hoare by whose permission they are shown here.

SAWYERS AT WORK
Most sawpits seem to have been holes in the ground; this picture shows the two sawyers at work planking a trunk of timber. The man at the bottom not only stood in the sawdust but did most of the work, being responsible for the cutting stroke!

THE SOWER

GATHERING MANGOL WURZELS
The man in the bowler hat is Mr. P. Stevens, his son Willie is on the right of the picture.

THE BLACKSMITH
Eber Trant, the local blacksmith, had his smithy at the back of Fore Street (opposite Lloyds Bank site).

Amongst those working on the house may be seen Tom Browning (highest on long ladder) and James Martin, painter and decorator (in doorway) together with three members of the Vincent family carpentry and joinery business — William (founder of the business in 1880, died 1921, aged 71 — left of doorway with back to camera), William Hedley (son, died 1951, aged 74 — father of R. W. H. Vincent, present Town Mayor — on shorter ladder), Herbert Fice (brother of W. H., local photographer as well as carpenter and joiner — far right on the family handcart). Names by R. W. H. Vincent.

TORR HILL HOUSE (probably about 1910)

TORR HILL
Later renamed "Uphill" this photograph shows Mr. J. J. Simpson, the owner (second from right) with the outside staff. From left to right: John Williams (labourer), W. Beer (coachman), J. Brooks (foreman), J. Yabsley (builder) and Robert Swan (gardener).

IVYBRIDGE SCHOOL

A church school was opened on 30th December, 1856, Mr. and Mrs. Mee being schoolmaster and mistress with a salary of £100 per annum. Later the school became a Board School under first the Ermington and then the Ivybridge School Board. By 1898 there was an average attendance of 172 boys and girls and 120 infants.

One of the best remembered headmasters was Mr. James Lake, who, appointed in 1873, served the school for 31 years. It was said at his retirement that he had educated the vast majority of people then living in Ivybridge and that more than 2,000 youngsters had passed through during his time.

An infants school class of about 1921. Amongst those who may be recognised are: Miss Love (left) and Miss Crees (right).
Back row: Ted Hurrell (2nd from left), Miss Hurrell (5 from l.), C. Roberts (2 from rt.). *2nd row:* R. Burton (3 from l.), L. French (4 from l.), G. Northmore (7 from l.), R. W. H. Vincent (in front of Miss Crees). *3rd row:* B. Williams (2 from l.), J. Yabsley (3 from rt.). *Front row:* (sitting): May Willcocks (rt. end). Identification and photo from Mr. Vincent.

SCENES OF LOCAL LIFE

IVYBRIDGE RUGBY TEAM 1895

Back row, from left: Dick Kitson, Ben Street, Archie Olver, George Lunnon, (a sailor), Bill Fry, Alec Lang. *Front row:* Duffer Symonds, Bill Hodge, Curly Browning, A. Curson, George Marshall, Abraham Pawley, — Curson, Sammy Daniels (absent Obo Vincent). Identifications, Mr. Hoare.

SCENES OF LOCAL LIFE

UNITY IS STRENGTH

A Friendly Society procession passing the Bridge Inn; sometime before the First World War.

IVYBRIDGE TOWN BAND

From left, *back row:* James Martin, Mr. Baskerville, Wm. Martin, —, —, *front row:* Jn. Martin Snr., Mr. Exworthy, Ned Blight, John Laing, —, —, —. Names by Mr. Hoare.

EARLY DAYS OF MOTORING

Mr. Charles Hoare sits proudly at the wheel of a 1907 Napier outside the entrance to Widecombe in the Moor church. Photograph about 1912. In 1920 the Ivybridge council got so concerned about traffic as to suggest a 7 m.p.h. speed limit!

AFTER THE WAR
Unveiling of the memorial to the men of Ivybridge who had fallen during the Great War by Lieut. Col. F. B. Mildmay, M.P., on 8th September, 1922.

ANYONE FOR A DRIVE?
A party in S. H. Lee's chara-banc, probably early 1920s. *Front:* Driver Freeman, Reg Calf, Charlie Broom, *2nd row:* Bessie Love (nee Browning), —, Mrs. Calf, Mr. Calf (railway signalman), *3rd row:* Mrs. Manley, Mr. Manley (tailor, Fore St.), Miss Coker, Mr. George Coker. Names by Mr. T. W. Maddock.

HUNTING
For many years Ivybridge has been the home of the Dartmoor Foxhounds seen here just before the First World War. Visitors would come down to stay in the town for the hunting season.

FORE STREET IN LATER YEARS

Fore Street and the Wesleyan chapel sometime in the 1930s. Some of the road traffic that in post-war years was to build up to an almost intolerable level can be seen.

A picture taken about 1952. The saddler's shop has now been demolished; Mr. Luxton's shop on the right remained almost unchanged until the 1970s.

Another picture of about the same time showing Town Dairy, Wayside Cafe, a Plympton Rural District Council dustcart and the old style pedestrian crossing.

AROUND THE VILLAGES
CORNWOOD

An extensive parish with a population of just over 1,000 at the turn of the century, there were two villages, Cornwood (or Cross) and Lutton, as well as ancient settlements such as Cholwich Town, Fardel, Hanger and Wisdome mostly dating from Domesday times. There were groups of cottages at Corntown, Tor and Yeo. The larger houses such as Blachford (the Misses Deare), Delamore (the Parkers), and Slade had a dominant influence on the village itself.

By 1906 the village counted a blacksmith, a wheelwright, a baker, a shopkeeper and post office amongst local trades together with china clay working by Martin Bros. and Watts, Blake & Bearne. The only inn was the Cornwood Inn, the corner of which is shown in the picture of the square. The second picture dates from 1925 but may well have been taken several years earlier.

LUTTON

Lutton (Ludeton) is described in 1906 as a hamlet of Cornwood. At this time there was an inn (the Mountain Inn), a Congregational chapel and "Cornwood and District Co-operative Society". The view dates from the early years of the century.

ERMINGTON

Ermington is a Saxon settlement that dates from about 700 A.D. and which gave its name to Ermington Hundred, one of the old administrative divisions of Devon. By the early years of this century the village boasted a post office, a school, a police station as well as numerous farmers, a tailor, a grocer and draper, two masons, dairymen, millers, a wheelwright, a baker and boot and shoemakers.

There were three inns in the village — the First and Last (F. Daniel), the Old Inn (F. Ford) shown in the first picture and now closed, and the New Inn (Mrs. Backhouse) now known as the Crooked Spire after that well known feature of the nearby parish church.

WRANGATON

Wrangaton, a hamlet in Ugborough parish, was the site of Kingsbridge Road station on the South Devon line. Passengers for Kingsbridge would alight here and travel by road until the opening of the branch line from South Brent. The station, which boasted a bookstall, was later renamed after the village but the hotel (shown in the picture) kept up the old name.

UGBOROUGH

Another Domesday village, Ugborough parish includes both Bittaford and Wrangaton as well as numerous farms and an area of moorland. The village square, shown in this photograph, is dominated by the parish church, St. Peter's, which lies in a prehistoric earthwork. By the time this picture was taken in the early years of the century the village contained a Congregational chapel, a reading room, a board school and a police station.

Amongst local trades, apart from those engaged directly in agriculture, were grocer and draper, blacksmith, miller, mason, shoemaker and builder as well as the two local inns, the Ship and the Anchor.

Ugborough fair was one of the great occasions of the year when swings and roundabouts were set up in the square. This view dates from 1907 and is looking down from in front of the church towards the school.

BITTAFORD

Bittaford or Bittaford Bridge was on the old turnpike road where it crossed the Lud brook and a toll house still stands in the village. By 1900 a settlement, as today dominated by the viaduct, had grown up and had both a post office and a Wesleyan chapel. The station ("platform") was opened in 1907. This view was before road widening and the old "Horse and Groom" back may be seen in the background.

The Horse and Groom (prop. H. R. White) as it was before the First World War on the opposite side of the road to the present building of that name. Road widening between the wars led to its demolition and rebuilding.

A view of "Blackadon", a name in common use for Plymouth Mental Hospital (now Moorhaven Hospital) even after its change of name from the original (1891) Plymouth Borough Asylum. Originally with six wards and 200 patients an extension was completed in 1905 to double the accommodation.

OLD IVYBRIDGE — Just Gone

Three pictures taken in the 1970s.

H. J. F. Lee's mill, demolished in a hurry by South Hams District Council.

Chapel Place before the restoration of the old chapel as a Town Hall and the demolition of the cottages.

Torrhill House (Uphill) just prior to demolition by a property developer after being allowed to fall into disrepair.

Arthur L. Clamp – the man behind the books

Arthur Leslie Clamp was a man of boundless energy with a passion for helping others, particularly through his love of history. A printer by trade, he started his career in a printing company before moving his family from Exeter to Plymouth to teach at the Plymouth College of Art and Design, where he eventually became the Head of the Printing Department.

A Devoted Family Man

Arthur with his five children.

Despite his love of teaching, Arthur prioritised his family, always making it home by 5:30pm for tea. He and his wife, Rosemary, raised five children: Susan, Angela, Elizabeth, David, and Steven. Arthur would often combine his love of family and history by taking his children on Sunday walks, encouraging them to appreciate historical monuments by taking photos or making crayon rubbings of gravestones for his books. The family home at 203 Elburton Road was a hub of activity, with a large garden, featuring a two-storey fort and a makeshift swimming pool.

A Lifelong Learner and Adventurer

Arthur's thirst for knowledge extended beyond history to a deep curiosity about the world. He was passionate about exploring different cultures, traditions, and cuisines, often taking advantage of his long summer holidays as a teacher to travel to places like India, Russia, South America, the middle east and the USA, sometimes bringing one of his children along. This adventurous spirit even influenced his home life, as seen by the short-lived family tradition of steam-cooking vegetables after a trip to Iceland.

History is a prominent feature of family days out

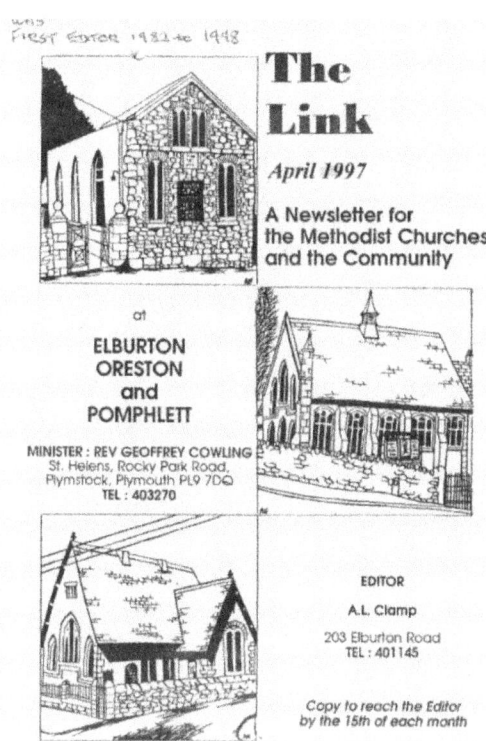

Community and Philanthropic Spirit

His commitment to serving others was evident in his long-standing involvement with the Elburton Methodist Church. He was the Sunday School Superintendent for over 15 years and served as the editor of the wider church's monthly newsletter, "The Link," for a similar duration. After Rosemary's very sad passing, Arthur later remarried and, following a chance encounter with a professor from India, established a connection with a missionary school in Chennai. Together with his new wife, Christine, he co-founded a "Sponsor a Child's Education" program that continues to this day.

Pictured left – The cover of 'The Link' complete with hand drawn sketches of each church by Angela
Below right – Arthur Clamp promoting his latest book
Below left – Arthur at home with his first wife, Rosemary
Below centre – Arthur on holiday with his second wife, Christine

A Legacy of Learning and Positivity

Arthur's greatest passion was history, which he brought to life through tireless research, documentation, and the many books he authored. He was driven by a need to "never be stuck in a rut," constantly seeking new experiences, meeting new people, and expanding his knowledge. With a positive attitude and a great sense of humour, he was always ready to help others, leaving a lasting impact on his family and community. His children, Susan, Angela, Elizabeth, David, and Steven, remember him with love and gratitude.

David Clamp, 2025

A Legacy of Local History

Below is the story of how Arthur L Clamp began writing books, in his own words, drafted shortly before he passed away in 2001. I have only made minor alterations to this text, correcting grammatical errors that he did not survive to correct himself. When I first discovered this text, I was shocked to see my name mentioned. It seems that, unbeknownst to me, I shared my first PC with him. I suspect he used it during the day when I was at school, although I do have one memory of sitting with him and showing him how it worked. It has been a pleasure to pick up where he left off and see his books republished and redistributed, and to know that I was part of the story, even back then. It was also fascinating to discover that his pricing structure matches the way I have tried to price the books, with a third going to local sellers and the rest covering printing costs with a little left over for my expenses.

I am his eldest grandson, and it is a privilege to curate his legacy, which we are calling 'The Clamp Collection'. The very last line of the text originally reads "The following pages list all the titles." Sadly, that page is missing and we have no record of all the books he published and knowing that some of those were researched by other authors makes the process of finding them even harder. I look forward to one day completing the collection and seeing them all available again. And maybe, one day, I'll even start writing my own to add to the series. For now, here is his story in his own words.

Steven Gibson, 2025

Writing and Publishing Booklets on Local Topics and Areas

I started this interest in either 1968 or 1969 when living in Woodford. I had by these dates established the Department of Printing and I think I must have been looking for something different to do. The first titles were of A5 size proofed from type set at Clarke, Doble and Brendon, Ltd., Plymouth printers, and then made up into pages and printed at Sawtell and Neilson, Ltd., Totnes.

Then began a slow process of getting them out to shops, etc. which proved to be more time consuming and difficult than actually researching, writing and getting the books into print. However, I persisted and opened a business account with Barclays Bank on the Broadway. I was advised to give it a title so I called it "Westway Publications". There came along another problem, one of storage of paper and finished books which was solved when the family moved to Elburton in 1970.

I changed the printer to Penwell, Ltd., Callington, Cornwall, as he was then just setting up himself and his prices seemed very reasonable. I did not get any of the printers to make up the complete books. I hand folded the flat printed sheets, stitched the books on a small manual table stitcher and trimmed them in a small hand turned guillotine which I bought from someone in Penzance for £40. It was brought up in a van.

The trouble and time going to and fro to Callington was too much so I transferred the printing to PDS Printers, Prince Rock, Plymouth, and I have been with them ever since. Now they are at Plympton which is easy to reach and they fold the flat sheets which was turning out to be a long chore which only saved a small part of the printing costs.

All my first titles were written by myself. I took the photographs and developed them in the loft of the house, the type was set by now on a computer situated in the house at Elburton from which I had collected photographic lengths of text to cut up and law down as pages.

At some point I decided that I would do my own film processing of lith film so I bought a large second hand process camera from Kingsbridge and learnt through trial and error to make line negatives of the text and halftone negatives of the illustrations which proved more difficult than I anticipated. The main problem was trying to keep the developer in the large dish at the correct temperature as any change would affect the developing time. I replaced this old camera with a brand new one bought from Croydon, Surrey, costing £900. This has turned out to be a great asset cutting out an expensive part of the printer's costs and one crucial aspect of the work which I could control.

By the middle 1970s there were many outlets I had contacted in Plymouth, up to Dartmoor, Exeter, around to Torbay, Totnes, Dartmouth and the South Hams. The market for local books was much greater than I had first thought and through getting to know many local people undertaking research themselves had the chance to help and make up books for other people who had in most instances, got together a collection of photographs with some text in a rather muddled way. Through my experience in print I was able to shape up their work and get it into print and in every case I had to pay the printer and let the person have the royalties. In the majority of titles produced in this manner this was another way of producing titles and it did give some profit to my work. However, I must say that in a few cases I lost out by either the other person getting the numbers wrong, not returning any monies from stock I delivered or they thought that more of their books should have been sold.

The print run was usually 1,000 copies and from time to time I have had reprints of 250 copies. It took about ten years to clear the first print run so I always had large stocks in the garage, workshop, etc. The numbers sold during the early years was about 7,000 copies a year increasing to around 9,000 copies and for the whole of the enterprise about 500,000 have been sold. The booklets have become part of the local scene and many people collect them, shops regularly order copies and I go around certain areas month by month restocking or replacing titles as necessary.

During the past year or so I have started setting the text on a Packard Bell PC, something which I should have done some years back. I share it with Steven Gibson, my grandson. There appears to be no end to the market for local books, but I could not earn a regular income because of the long time it takes to sell stock.

However, now exceeding 100 titles made up mainly of A4 twenty-four page booklets, some folded guides, with selling prices set with a third going to the shop which is the trade custom, the original idea has been quite successful and could go on for ever.

Apart from monetary benefits, however spasmodically these might be, I have learnt a lot myself, met many interesting people and have become part of the local scene with requests to give talks and to advise people about getting into print.

Arthur L Clamp, 2001

This newspaper article, published by the Evening Herald on 17th August 2001, forms a good record of his life. Just as he encourages us to learn more about local history, we encourage you to learn a little about him. For that reason, we have included these pages at the back of all the most recently republished books, in honour of his memory and recognition of his contribution to the community.

www.ingramcontent.com/pod-product-compliance
Lightning Source LLC
Chambersburg PA
CBHW061408070526
44584CB00031B/4186